APA FORMATTING 7TH EDITION

NEWEST EDITION

The Easy Guide to APA Referencing

By

Emily Grace

Table of Contents

Introduction

In October 2019, the APA published another version of its publication manual called the 7th Edition. This new Edition replaced the 6th Edition published in 2009; this shows that the 7th Edition is better than the old one. TIME has passed since 2009 till now. New knowledge is gained, and technology has advanced rapidly, making new developments possible. Citing online material has developed more, and it's better than before and the use of bias-free language compared to 2009.

This manual contributes value to some specific sectors in the industry such as writers, students, social sciences, etc. Because of this new Edition, more research is now possible for reference and recitation techniques at any time. APA also regulates the manner, language, document type, in-text excerpts, and references.

This manual offers much guidance in choosing titles, figures, and vocabularies in publications, resulting in a high standard, solid and educative communication in many known and unknown sectors. This manual has helped many users to acquire adequate writing methods, from authoring to conducting research, report making, and giving reviews through publications.

This latest Edition is an essential means of support for students and professionals to accomplish distinction, eminence, and superiority in their publications, thereby making a global impact that can trend for a long time. This Edition has the potential of eclipsing the successes of the last Edition.

Purpose Of The 7th Edition
This manual aims to make characteristic differences between certain formatting elements for educational sector uses over publications.

Two Main Reasons For Using APA
1. It is the only upgraded consistent format writers can use any time they want to write a publishing article.

2. This manual helps writers to organize their work effectively.

Moreover, why Is APA So Important
3. It provides a more apparent quality to articles with incredibly complex ones.

4. It makes your writing easier to comprehend when reading.

5. Like I said above, it helps writers to organize their work efficiently.

6.   It also helps the reader to spot important information quickly, which is essential while evaluating your research.

7.   It provides an upgraded and consistent format for writers to use.

For your writings to have intellectual efficacy in APA publications, they must have the following parts in

them.

8.   The title page is a crucial page that covers the paper's heading, the author's name, and an institute affiliation.

9.   Abstract - this is the summary of your publication. You can read more about the abstract in chapter three of this e-book.

10.   Introduction – this is where you talk about your key points in detail. Use one or two paragraphs to make your issues effective.

11.   A literature review is a typical summary review of what you say in a given topic or question. A good literature view has this formation:

1.   Introduction

2.   Thesis statement

3.   Summarization and detailed resources

4.   Order of references

5.   Method- this is easy to write but has to be carefully examined when writing. The reason for this is to detail all you have registered so that anyone can easily copy your work without thinking twice.

6.   Results – it summarizes every information that was gathered and carefully describes what was done on the paper.

7.   Discussion – this is when you think and explain better your ideas in your paper. You can make out of it your thoughts and your final statements about the article from this.

8.   Conclusion – This is the last paragraph of your paper where you summarize the ideas you have used on the form. Whether you approve or disapprove of anything in other sections.

9.   Reference etc.

You might not use them all, but you can use most of them to present your work efficiently on paper. The importance of the above gives you report and improves your proficiency as a writer,

10.   Credibility –It is an undeniable authentication in your writing career.

11.   It also gives you protection from allegations of plagiarism when you use APA citation essential.

However, the importance of this manual cannot be overemphasized. It changed a lot of setbacks when it came to the old Edition. Many might disagree because they are used to the old Edition and are afraid to try something new. This manual has been tested and found to be trustworthy by the APA before it is recommended. This Edition is currently the best version because its features are unique and superior to the older Edition.

Furthermore, it is advised to consult the newest Edition when working on a topic. Suppose you have twenty authors that are involved in your publication. In that case, the best option will be to go for the latest version because its capacity is extended to contain more names, unlike the previous version that can only contain seven characters at the maximum.

Next, when writing using the latest 7th version of the manual, you can write out the name of the website used plainly, and after a while, the URLs will show, but in the older Edition, only the URLs shows and no website is included in publications. The latest Edition's significant changes are that references remove the publisher's name, articles should have an issue number, making it easy to locate the sources, etc.

Finally, this Edition will be available this spring 2020, and Ithaca must get it. You can see how it looks by looking above. If you haven't used any editions and probably want to get the latest one, it's orange in color, but the 6th Edition is all-around blue.

And if you want to convert from the 6th Edition to the 7th Edition.

1. Open your current Edition, which happens to be the 6th version.

2. Copy the contents of your write-up.

3. Start a new paper using the PERRLA Add-in and use the title page information for the latest version of the APA Manual.

4. Press command +V (Mac) on the keyboard and paste the copied text into the new version.

5. Include sources from the reference library into the PERRLA side window. The method takes you to update & add the contacts in the new Edition.

Remember
When done with the steps mentioned above, recreate your citations for easy connection with the newest edition format.

CHAPTER ONE

Page Layout

Page layout shows how each page on your paper will be like when printed. This layout will tell the writer's thoughts, organization skills, and delivery, so your page layout must be presentable. If you have a scattered page layout, no reader will love to read your paper. Let your presentation be one of the things that readers love about you. Let it be something that can single you out among others.

Throughout your paper, you need to include this guideline in your writing

1. Margins- it's a space at the side of a written or printed page, so make sure you use one margin and not 2 for the entire page or write-up. It will make your writing look organized to the reader.

2. Use an indent for every paragraph and footnote, doing your writing not further away from the edge of the page than the other line.

3. ½ from the left margin, use indent set-off quotations.

Text Formatting

4. Text font- This should be easily obtainable to every user. There are various font categories, namely Serif fonts, Sans Serif, Script, and display fonts.

5. Don't change from one front to another. Use the same font for the whole paper to avoid disorganizing your writing.

6. Use fonts like San serif for online writings than other Fonts like Calibri, Arial on 11 points, or Lucida sans Unicode on 10pt for further report.

7. If you want to publish works, I propose Times New Roman or Georgia each on 12 and 11 points, respectively. Use serif fonts also.

8. Font magnitude and category exceptions- Figure images utilize the serif fonts with a type size between 8 to 14. This kind of size makes it simpler to read without eye strains.

9. Computer code- use monospace fonts—this time with Lucida console or courier new all on 10pt.

10. Footnotes- use default footnotes setting of words

11. Do not use hyphenation- this means connecting syllables and words by hyphens, making it hard to comprehend the writing.

Page Header

It is located at the top margin of every page on a paper. When it comes to the student paper, the page header has only a page number, number 1, and it is written or found at the right top corner of your page while the professional paper comprises page number and running head at the top left corner of your page.

CHAPTER TWO

Title Page

A title page is a requirement for all APA-style manuscripts. There are two types of title manuscripts, and they include

1. The student and

2. Professional documents.

Students use the version suitable for them, while professionals use it only when the instructor or institute demands a different version of their paper. Students' version was designed to help students to create their title pages.

Student Title Page

A student paper is the type of manuscript required from or given to only students or an institute.

Students titled pages consist.

- The title of the page.

- The names of the authors.

- The affiliation of the author(s):

- The name of the tutor

- Course number

- Name of the paper recipient

- Page number

- Assignment deadline

Let's See An Illustration Below.
Students' paper does not require a running head except if the tutor or a school asks for it.

These guides shown below in a table form helps to form the student's title version needed.

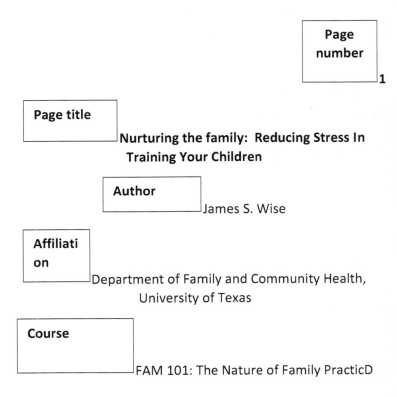

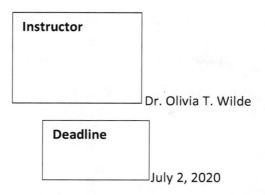

Instructor

Dr. Olivia T. Wilde

Deadline

July 2, 2020

Professional Title Page

This type of paper is required or given to by a professional body like organizations.

This version consists of the manuscript title, writer name, writer affiliation, writer note, running head, and the page number.

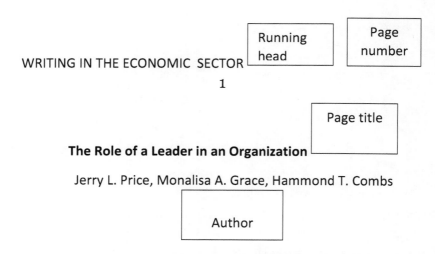

Running head

Page number

WRITING IN THE ECONOMIC SECTOR

1

Page title

The Role of a Leader in an Organization

Jerry L. Price, Monalisa A. Grace, Hammond T. Combs

Author

Department of Sociology, Orange County College

Center for Human Growth and Culture, University of Florida

Department of Sociology, Brown University

Institute for Behavioral Research, University of Florida

Affiliations

Author's Note

Monalisa .A. Grace http://org/000.666-555-321

Hammond .T. Combs http://org/000/323-123-332

Jerry L. Price stays at Social Science Department

Department of Sociology, Orange County College

We have all that we need. Thank you

Any other information concerning this paper should be presented to Jerry L. Prince.

Chicago University, 56 Downton Abbey Publishers, CA 13213 Email

Authors note

Jlp@gmail.com

Let's see an illustration below.

The guidelines below show the format in table form with parts how a professional type looks like,

Professional Format	Illustration
title page forum	
Paper title	When you get to your page, carefully write down the title of your work by counting two to three lines down. Center it in the middle with bold font and type. Write in a capital letter the main word, which is the title. Write down the label, including the subtitle, separately with double-line spacing required. When it comes to titles, don't abbreviate but	Known and unknown: known Errors that Disapprove Fraud In Nigeria

state well the name of your tag on paper, also Include important words needed.

| Author names | Position one doubled space line under the name and the writer's names for an easy read. Write down the author's name carefully on separate lines. If there is more than one author on the page, use "and "to separate the two names but if they are three or more authors on the page, use the comma to | Judy Rulford Clark |

separate one name from the other except for the last name; use the word "and."

If various writers have different collaborations, use superscript numerals after each writer's name for proper connection to relevant affiliations. Still, if authors have the same afflictions, there will be no need for superscript numerals.

Rosemont Kelly

David Cole

Mercy Great

Blair John Page

Author Affiliation

For this type of paper, affiliation is the

Department of Sociology,

college, also write out the department and college name and separate them with a comma. After the author's name, write the affiliation next to the double-spaced line.

If many authors have affiliations, use the numeral numbering after each author's name to connect to relevant associations properly. Still, if authors have the same afflictions, there will be no

Brown University

1

Department of Psychology,

Yale University

2

Department of family and community health sciences,

	need for superscript numerals.	University of California
Author note	Outline the author's note at the bottom part of your page.	n/a
	boldly write at the center the label "Author Note" make sure that his note is aligned to the left side	
Running head	It must appear in capital letters in the page header of all the pages, including the title page. Make sure that your running head is always aligned on the left side. Do	KNOWN ERRORS THAT DISAPPROVE FRAUD IN NIGERIA.

	not use the labeling	
Page number	Use the number on the title page for easy identification. Go to your page numbering column in your Microsoft word and insert the number on the top right corner of your page.	1

CHAPTER THREE

Abstract

An abstract is a summary of your paper. It is one of the most critical sections that is highly needed when writing a paper. You don't joke around with the abstract of your paper, and you don't write it anyhow. The abstract is usually brief, but it is written for easy understanding of your paper. It will help the reader to see your stand-out points before reading your entire paper. Every paper, exceptionally professional papers, needs an abstract except students' papers.

This abstract gives a reader a reason to read your paper or not. Your abstract should not be too extended, or else it will be a bore for the reader. All you need to do is make sure your points are solid, catchy for the eyes, and understandable to the mind giving your paper an edge in your writing career, making your work unique and Powerful. It tells the reader what to expect. This expectation creates suspense in the mind of your reader. With this, they can go all the way with your paper.

Your abstract should not be longer than 250 words, so take your time and choose your words carefully. Let your abstract also begins on its page and not with the rest of the topics. Do not stress your reader by going through your page looking for something to catch his attention. Let your abstract be soul appealing, and let it be in-between your cover page and the first chapter of your paper. Let it be the first thing that welcomes your reader into your mind.

How your abstract should be like

1. Describe what your paper is all about. Make it bold and simple. No long stories because you will have the time to tell us what methods you used to write your paper. The reader will know what type of paper he should expect.

2. If it is important to you, it will be essential to your reader. What are the things that strikeout differently for you?

3. When you finalize the paper, it will hit differently to the reader if there were a lesson to be seen and experienced or not.

Mistakes that most people make while writing an abstract

1. Not summarising in the abstract – this summary is essential and unique in its way. Without it, the reader will not know what to expect in your paper. There should be something that will make your reader want to read other chapters in your book.

2. If your abstract is way too long- an extended abstract should be avoided at all costs. Don't be tempted to give us everything in the abstract instead, give us a tease about your book. It will make it more exciting to read your paper. An extended abstract is a red flag so avoid it, or else your readers will prevent you and your book.

3. When your abstract lacks points – valid points in the abstract should not be taken likely. Without enough

facts to convince your reader to read your book, then you just wasted your time writing an uninteresting paper for nobody. Be enticing with your words, and your reader will read your article with excitement.

4. Using abbreviations- this makes your reader not know what you want to say. They can't read minds, so write your words plainly to understand what you want to say. We don't assume when writing. We clarify when writing.

5. Adding up information on the paper may not be easy, but it is necessary to stick to your plan. Your valid points are more important than another idea. Adding another thing to your abstract will be a distraction when the reader starts reading your paper. That is to say, "you wrote out of point."

6. Disobedience to specific instructions- if you don't follow a particular guideline given to you for your work, your paper will be returned by your or corrections, so follow due process, and your paper will get approval for publications.

7. Failure to use critical words- keywords are an essential part of your abstract. It makes your paper quickly approved and accessible by anyone looking for material for work. Some writers think that it is unimportant. Keywords promote your work quickly.

Keep in mind that as a writer, never assume your reader knows what you know. Don't assume that every published paper out there has a good abstract. It's possible because they never had a good editor to edit their writing. Lastly, Ask for a review of your work before you publish it. With an editor with a good eye, you will be a readable writer.

CHAPTER FOUR

Contents for APA 7th Edition Manual are

1. Reference and in-text quotations in APA Style

2. Extensive use of words.

3. APA Paper layout

4. Mechanics of style

5. APA 7th publication reference generator

6. Available study slides

7. Acquiring the new 7th publication of the APA Manual

8. Questions

Citations and in-text citing in APA Style

In sources citing expeditions, there are road maps that can help you during your research. These road maps have been given to rectify some past mistakes and future possibilities in writing.

There are so many examples that have has been given already, from books to audiovisuals, including social media, etc., to make citing sources easier. In each category, easy templates have been made available for comprehension and the proper application.

The publisher's location is not contained in the citation anymore. For example

1. Dedaly, G.T. (2012). The two kinds of family in our society. Texas, TX: David &Daniel

2. Dedaly, G.T. (2012). The two kinds of family in our society. David &Daniel

1. **The in-text reference for manuscripts with three or additional writers is now short penned compared to before. from the onset of the initial citation, you only inscribe the writer's first title and "1st al".** for example

1. **Before** (Harper, Johnson, Charles, &Gaye, 2015)

2. **Now** (Harper et al., 2015)

3. **Up to 15 authors (instead of 6), initials, and surnames should be in the reference record.**

1. Gave, T. V, Brown, Mary Ezekiel G., L. I Vase, C.A. Bassett, G.F. Bassey... Bird, G. T (2014)

2. Have, T. V, Brown, Mary Ezekiel G, L. I Vase, C.A. Bassett, G.F. Bassey, Brown H.B, Angela T.O, Eric D.D. , James Jane H., Harmony U.H., York G. E., Levine, Devon H.C, . . . Bird, G. T (2014).

3. **DOIs are formatted similarly to URLs. The tag " DOI:" is outdated.**

1.   DOI:

      10.1242/20054355.2015. 3216542

2.   http://doi.org/ 10.1242/20054355.2015.3216542

3.   **URLs_do not come before "Retrieved from,"
      except it is required. The title of the website is
      added unless it's the same as the writer's own.**

      1.   Reelcreek, T. (2018,October 14). APA   7th
            edition: The most visible changes [Blog post].
            Retrieved from

            https://www.scribbr.com/apa-   style/   apa-
            seventh-edition- changes/

      2.   Reelcreek, T. (2018, October 14). APA 7th
            Edition: The most visible changes. Scribbr.

            http://www.scribbr.com/ apa- style/ apa-
            seventh- edition- changes/

4.   **E-books, platforms, the format, or devices are
      no more in the reference, and the publisher is
      added.**

      1.   Burke, N. (2008). Evolution of man in the
            beginning: Scientist and Anatomy [Kindle
            version].

            http:/doi.org/11.1000/543-34-121-2811-1

2.   Burke, N. (2008). Evolution of man in the beginning: Scientist and Anatomy. Springer Nature.

http:/doi.org/11.1000/543-34-121-2811-1

5.   Clear written guidelines are made available for contributors more than writers. For example, the host should be added; for a TV series, both the writer and the director should be cited.

6.   Many illustrations are used by online sources such as YouTube videos, social media platforms, etc. Most times, hashtags and emoticons are usually defined when used.

Inclusive and bias-free language

Nowadays, writing with so vast a knowledge we have now and without partiality towards a group of people, and APA's newest 7th edition manual has a separate chapter on this. These materials given by APA have helped writers reduce being partial, especially in specific topics like age, sex, languages, etc., some go as far as being racial to particular individuals. Without this knowledge, there will be labeling among individuals to a certain level. Some illustrations are

7.   The singular " they " is publicly accepted as a sex pronoun.

1.   A writer's job lies in how well they are cited.

2.   A writer's job lies in how well they are cited.

8.   Descriptive phrases are better than an adjective to label a particular group of people.

  1.   The sick

  2.   People are living in sickness.

9.   Using the same age ranges is more relevant than broad groups.

  1.   Children over 15 years old

  2.   Children with the age bracket of 15 to 20 yrs.' old

Mechanics of style
Few changes have been made in the newest Edition.

The updated guidelines are better detailed in two known changes:

10.   In linguistic examples, use double quotation marks instead of italics.

  1.   APA uses a singular pronoun they

  2.   APA uses the singular noun "they."

CHAPTER FIVE

HEADINGS

A heading, also called a **running head**, is employed to direct a reader through a text; it identifies the main contents and points out important features. It is usually written in capital letters. With a short and precise heading, a reader can expect main points to keep track of other development.

A heading appears with the top margin of a paper along with the page number.

A heading should not have more than fifty characters, including punctuation and spacing. Properly formatted headings assist readers of various abilities. Headings are organized according to their level of inferiority.

To arrange the parts within the body of a paper, APA has five various levels of headings. These levels can be characterized by what an outline has and how Roman numerals are attached to the main topics, capital letters to the subtopics, etc. Generally, each section of the publication should begin with a level one heading.

The first paragraphs of a text are usually understood to be introductory; therefore, the heading "introduction" is not essential. A writer can use headings within the introduction, but it is not required. Within the introduction, level two headings are for the first subsection, level three for any subsection under the level two heading, and so on. In the main section of the text, after the introduction, a level one heading is used.

In a text, the number of headings used is contingent on the difficulty and length of the work. The writer should use Level one headings if only one level of heading is needed, Level two headings if two Levels of headings are required, etc. To particularize unique sections in a paper, make use of the numbers of headings significant

In addition, writers should avoid common mistakes associated with headings, such as:

Having just one subsection within a section
Characterization of headings with numbers and letters
Switching to the single spacing within headings instead of maintaining a double spacing
Addition of blank lines above or below a heading, even if it is at the end of a page
Not making use of title case, that is; upper and lower case letters

In consideration of the addition of headings, APA instructs that a writer should only add a header if two or more subsections use the same level of heading. A heading is not mandatory for all papers; Long and formal reports should have headings, especially when starting with an Abstract; short student papers may not need headings.

There are five levels of heading and how they are formatted;

- Centered, Bold type, Uppercase, and lowercase headings: Start the text on a new line in a fresh paragraph
- Left-aligned, Bold type, Uppercase, and Lowercase headings: Start the text in a new line in a new section.
- Left-aligned, Bold type, Italicized, Upper and Lower case heading: Start the text as a fresh line in a new paragraph.
- Indentation, Bold type, Upper and Lower case heading Ended with a period: Start the text on the same line as the heading and proceed as a typical paragraph.
- Indentation, Bold type, Italicized, Upper and Lower case heading and climaxing with a Period: Start the text on the same line as the heading and continue as a regular paragraph.

The seventh(7th) edition of APA style is the latest; it uses only three levels of heading: level three, four, and five headings. APA updated levels three to five to enhance readability. All headings are written now in the subject case; essential words are in capital letters and boldface. Headings are now differentiated only by italicization, indentation, and the use of periods. In the 7ᵗʰ Edition, headings are necessary for only documents that will be submitted for publication.

A writer who utilizes the APA style can use the mechanized heading function of his word processing program to create headings. This feature ensures that headings are infused correctly in any electronic version of the paper and makes formatting headings simple, which benefits readers who use navigation tools.

Headings are used for organizing ideas within a text effectively. It establishes a hierarchy and highlights important topics within sections of the complete text.

Some changes were recommended on the topic of headings. The changes include the following:

- Headings are no longer needed when putting down student articles

- Professional papers should encompass a running head on every page, including the title page. This observation is only applicable to the 6th Edition, though, as the 7th Edition does not use title heads. Perhaps subsequent editions will review it.

- When it comes to abstracts and reference lists, they must follow the rules for all level one headings

- The rules regarding the styles of headings are no longer as strict as they used to be. The guidelines for writing fonts have been loosened a bit. This is done to accommodate the different styles and specifications of different computers.

CHAPTER SIX

In-text Citations

An in-text citation is the concise form of the reference included in the body of a text. It gives sufficient information to identify the peculiar origin in your reference list; it usually consists of the writer's family name and the year of publication; regardless of whatever a writer is referencing, an in-text citation will look the same.

In-text citation can either be in narrative or parenthetical form. **(Author, date)**, form in parentheses is the general form for sources, for example

as seen in a recent study (Williams and Smith, 2021) and discussed at great length in past years' literature (Shell, 2020).

There are essential guidelines to follow when writing the in-text citations; here are a few below:

- Ensure that the author's name in the parentheses and the name in the reference list are the same.
- Put only manuscripts that have been read and concept that has been absorbed into your writing. The work cited provides fundamental background knowledge to support or debate your theory or offer evaluative facts and meaning.

- Cite primary sources when feasible, and cite secondary sources sparingly.

- Cite sources to record all facts statistics mentioned in your text that are not common knowledge

- To cite a specific part of a source, provide an author-date citation for the work and information about the particular point.

- When a writer cannot retrieve sources, still give credit to the author in the text but avoid using sources that cannot be recovered.

- A reader might find a long string of citations hard to comprehend, mainly because they use assistive technology. For that reason, include only citations essential to support your immediate point.

In the 7th Edition of the APA style, In-text citation explains to readers where pieces of materials sourced outside your thoughts are gotten. The in-text citation is clearer when quoted straight from the source; it is required when a writer has recapitulated or rephrased from a source. When writing, to avoid plagiarism, every word and idea must be cited that they are gotten from somewhere else.

APA makes use of a combination of writer, date referencing methods. In this method, the writer adds both the writer's title and date within the text's body and adds a comparable reference in the reference list. This referencing method helps the reader to recognize sources used in a write-up by analyzing the writer and date inside the text of the paper and easily places the corresponding reference in the alphabetically arranged reference list.

When it comes to In-text citations, there are two categories that can be used within an APA publication that helps the reader to find the corresponding reference list. The two categories are **Narrative citation** and **Parenthetical citation instead of** footnotes that add the information's details under a page or an endnote where information is added at the end of the paper itself.

A narrative citation: is a citation in which the writer's title is used in the text of the sentence. After the writer's name is written, it is followed the year in parentheses; **Smith (2001) completed research on breast cancer and its treatments.** The writer's name and date can also be penned in the sentence without being in parentheses; *In 2001, Smith completed research on breast cancer and its treatments.* The year should be removed for various narrative citations in a single paragraph, and the date added at the end of the sentence.

A parenthetical citation is where the writer and the date are written in parenthesis and separated by a comma. It can appear within the body of the sentence or the sentence's conclusion. Suppose the reference is cited at the end of the sentence, place punctuation after the closing parentheses;

(author, date). Ensure that the information in parentheses is in line with the citation in the reference list.

When a quote is less than forty words, quotation marks are added to the quoted words. If the sources have designated page numbers, the writer and the date are written in the sentence as narrative citation, then the page number is added in parentheses at the end of the quote. If it doesn't have a designated page number, then a combination of both the paragraph number and writer is added.

When the quote is over forty words, put it in a block text. Do this by starting the quote on a new line, make an indentation of zero point five(0.5) inch from the left margin; for an additional paragraph within the quote, indent another zero point five (0.5) inch in. Do not add quotation marks and double-space the whole quotation block. After the selection, add a period after the last word in the sentence, then followed by the parentheses.

CHAPTER SEVEN

Quotations

A quote is a piece of text that has been copied directly from a source and included in a document. A quote can be a word, phrase, sentence, or an entire passage.

Quotations are used to extract or reference text from a source and added to the project being worked on.

There are general rules that must be adhered to when quoting in APA style:

- Insert the quote in double quotation marks if quoting less than 40 words

- Format it as a single blockquote when quoting more than 40 words

- Include the name of the author, year, and page number when citing a quote.

- Use "p." or "pp." when referencing a page or a range of pages

There are mainly two types of quotations; the long and the short quotations.

Short Quotations

When a quote is directly from the source, the writer's name, the year it was published, and the page number should be included.

If only a single page is referenced, the page number should be preceded by "p.", but if more than a single page is referenced, the range of the pages should be preceded by " pp.".

For example:

John(2004) said quotations and citations must be included at the end of the document (pp. 6-8).

Quoting a citation that includes the writer's name, year, and page number can become before a single phrase that introduces the sentence or paragraph, followed by the year of publication in parenthesis.

For example:

John(2004) introduced the concept of quotations (p.5) that their importance can never be over-emphasized.

In a case where the writer doesn't wish to include the writer's title in the same text with the sentence, the writer's last name, year of publication, and page number should be placed in parenthesis right after the quotation.

For example:

He stated in his book that "citations and quotations are a great way to detect and avoid plagiarism" (John, 2004, p.7)

Long Quotations

Long quotations are quotations that are used when the text to be quoted contains more than 40 words. In this case, the text is placed directly under the preceding text in a stand-alone block of text known as block quotes. The text begins on a new line.

When referencing long quotes, double quotation marks, as in the case of the short quotation, should not be used.

Begin the text on a new line and indent the first line of any subsequent paragraphs a half an inch from the left margin under the original indentation.

Be careful to maintain the format chosen and remain consistent throughout the work. Maintain double-spacing all through, and do not put in an extra vacant line ahead or after the quotation.

The parenthetical reference should appear after the ending punctuation mark.

For example:

This is a block of text that will be used to illustrate how a long quotation works. It is not difficult to understand because it is plain and easy to see. Once you understand the basic concept, you'll never experience any difficulty again.

John(2004) says that quotations and citation go hand in hand; whatever sources have been quote must also be cited.

(This should go on for all words above 400. Always maintain the   indentation for as long as the blockquote goes on.)

Quoting a Source Without Page Numbers
Some sources that are gotten from the internet or audiobooks have no page numbers. This may have been a thing to worry about, but this is no longer a problem with the APA 7th edition style of citation.

An alternative locator should be included when citing a direct quote for such sources, especially for sources referenced from the internet. URLs are long, thus the need for employing the alternate locator, except if the URL is very short. The shorter, the better.

The alternative locator could be the heading of a section, the number of a paragraph, a combination of the two, or another identification source. This identifier should be something **logical** and not abstract.

For example:

James(2010) says quotations from sources without page numbers should be logical and should begin the paragraph. (Para 4).

For other sources besides the URL of a webpage on the internet, sources such as Youtube videos, audiobooks, or movies, these sources have provisions for timestamps. Use these timestamps as an alternative locator to locate the beginning of the quote.

Note:

A corresponding citation and reference should be observed on a page after the documents are completed whenever a quotation is done.

CHAPTER EIGHT

Reference List

When it comes to a reference list, it is the total list of all the cited and used sources within the document. The reference list contains all in-text references and is located at the end of the document.

Its heading should read "References," and it should be centered on a new page. Its purpose is to give all the essential evidence that a reader needs and to offer it in a sequential way that is easier to understand.

It is also used to check the accuracy of sources used and also to detect and avoid plagiarism.

Tips For Creating a Reference List

- A reference list should begin on a fresh page. Its heading should read "References" and should be centered on top of the page

- All references should be included alphabetically, from A-Z, regardless of their format (whether books, journal articles, or online sources)

- The references should be ordered alphabetically, starting with the writer's surname

- A writer should list sources with no available author by the letter of the initial vital statement of the title

- Use 5-7 spaces to indent when the referencing exceeds one line

- Use dual spacing

- All references should end with a full stop. This rule is only exempted for references that end with a URL or DOI (Digital Object Identifier), which is a different and permanent identification number that links directly to a source on the internet.

Before seeing examples of how some common publications are cited, it is worthy not to mention that the 7th edition of the APA referencing style brought about some changes compared with the 6th Edition. Some of the differences include:

- In the 7th Edition, up to 20 authors should be written while citing. For sources with more than 20 authors, ensure to replace the name (s) of any author(s) after the 19th author with ellipses followed by the title of the last writer.

Note: there should be an ampersand (&) before the title of the last writer.

- DOIs and URLs are currently both presented as hyperlinks for electronic citations. Where the label "DOI" was once used, it is no longer used for entries that include a DOI.

In the 7th Edition, the phrase "Retrieved from" is only used when the date of retrieval is included in the citation.

How to Make a Reference List
Referencing a Journal Article

- Start with the name of the author(s) succeeded by the first initials

- The year it was published should be added in brackets

- The article's title should be written in italics

- The journal's title should be written in italics

- Do NOT write the volume of the journal in italics.

- Do NOT write the issue of the journal in italics.

- Also, make sure to include the page range of the article.

- DOIs should be inserted as hyperlinks that will lead directly to the quoted text

- The initial line of each citation is left-adjusted. All the other successive should be indented 5-7 spaces as in a paragraph.

- When referencing the title of books or referencing articles, or reports, or other sources, just the initial letter of the first statement of the title and subtitle, the first phrase after a colon or a dash in the title, and proper nouns.

- The general structure is the name of the author. First initial, (date). Title of the journal article. Title of journal. Issue of the journal (volume), date of issue. Link to journal

For example:

Jonah. C (2010). The Journey to Health. General Health Journal. 26(8), 21-23. Https//linktojournal.com

Referencing a Book
- Start by writing the writer's surname succeeded by the first initials

- A year of publication should be included in the bracket.

- Write the title of the book in italics

- If the book being referenced is the First Edition, the Edition should be not be included in round brackets. If it is not the first Edition, then brackets are necessary to encase the Edition of the book.

- The initial line of each citation should be left adjusted, and all other subsequent lines should be indented 5-7 spaces.

The general format of referencing a book is:

The surname of the writer, First initials (publication year). *Title of book in italics* (Edition). Publisher

For example:

Judas, D.J. (1997). *Betrayal is not cheap* (4th Edition). Nazareth Publishers

Referencing a Website
- The format for referencing a website is:

Last name of the writer, followed by initials. (Year, month date) Title of page or organization. Source.

Note:

- if the author is unknown, the name of the organization should be properly spelled out

- the date should be the last date the web article was updated.

- the source should be the official name of the website or the author

CHAPTER NINE

Footnotes

Footnotes and appendices are provisions made by additional spaces where some extra and valuable information may be shared within a document. Footnotes offer brief insights about certain points and paragraphs in the document, which may be long and detailed. The footnote of a page offers a quick overview of the format of the content with regards to the whole content. These little notes can be used to navigate and provide clarity on a subject. Footnotes are the supplementary details printed at the end of the page as relating to a paper's content or Copyright information. Its sole aim is to provide clarity and support the body paragraphs.

Footnotes are generally associated with Chicago notes Biblio style, and other styles use them sometimes. The 7th Edition of the APA style rarely uses footnotes, and they are only seen where it is absolutely necessary, and even when it is vital, it should be kept short and simple.

Footnotes are broadly divided into two main types: the content footnote and the copyright footnote. The content footnote is used to provide extra information about the source or direct a reader to another chapter. The copyright footnote is used to include copyright material that exceeds fair usage policy. This is rare but possible.

Footnotes are typically located at the bottom of a page after the page's contents have been typed out.

The two types of footnotes, content-based footnotes and footnotes that acknowledge Copyright, are discussed below:

Content-Based Footnotes
Employing footnotes to provide supplementary details can pad and enrich the text contained in the body and reinforce the paper's main points. Content-based footnotes may also be used to direct readers to a different source where they can obtain more details on the topic.

They should not be used to mislead readers, but they would provide directed and useful information. Footnotes should not be too long and boring but should be made as interesting as possible while providing the necessary information.

To acknowledge Copyright
Give credit to who credit is due. Copyright information should be credited in the footnote regardless if it is images, tables, a long quotation, or data of any form. It should be accurate and properly stated to avoid any form of plagiarism.

Copyright is needed for directly reporting as well as content that has been adapted. These portions of the document may require the express permission of the original author; this acknowledging said author will dissolve any legal battles in the future.

How to Format Footnotes

Each footnote and the callout it corresponds to in the text should be formatted in the form of numbers. It follows serially in order of appearance, and it uses superscripts.

For example:

My name is Josiah[1]. I am a man[2].

Footnotes

[1] name of a person

[2] gender

Note:

- Footnotes should not be placed in headings or in the middle of a paragraph. They are strictly placed at the end of the page. There should be no space between a callout and its corresponding number with the superscript.

- To avoid repetition and to reintroduce a footnote that has already been made functional (called out), do not duplicate. It should not be written twice. Instead, write it as: "See footnote 3," for example.

Positions of a footnote

- A footnote should be written at the foot of the page on which the correspondent callout is referenced. A footnote whose correspondent callout is on page 59 should also be on page 59. Do not shift the footnotes of a callout to a different page.

- Alternatively, a footnote can be created to follow the reference page. It should have a title written at the top center of the page, which will provide all the footnotes used in the document and their corresponding callouts.

In using this method, the page's title should be "Footnotes," which should be centered and bold. The footnotes should be recorded as a double-spaced and indented paragraph.

The superscripted number should be placed in front of each footnote and separate the numbers from the text that follows with a single space.

To format the information of Copyright, providing credit for texts obtained from other sources, including images, tables, figures, an accreditation statement at the end of the note for visual elements. For long quotations and questionnaires, the accreditation should be positioned at the foot of the page.

Below is the format of depicting footnotes for a journal article:

[1] From " Title of article," by the author's first name then by the first initials, year of Edition, the volume of the journal, the copyright year, and name of the copyright owner. Reprinted (or modified with permission).

CHAPTER TEN

Lists

Making Lists in writing help the readers understand some key points within a sentence. It is important to have your items in syntactic and abstract correspondence when creating a list. To better understand this, all items in a list might start with a phrase that starts with a verb, or better yet, all items must begin with a noun. To give more attention to details, American Psychological Association (APA) allowed the use of the lettered list, bulleted lists, and numbered lists.

When writing academic materials, it is likely that the writer would reference the work of others; it is important that the reference citation is properly documented. Referencing is the formal documentation of work that makes it acceptable for academic intentions. Just as there are guidelines when making reference citations, there are also guidelines for listing key points in an academic paper.

Types of Lists

APA offers guidance on how to properly make a paper qualify as an academic work. One of the guidance that APA offer is on the area of work listing. Since the initial Edition of the APA formatting method, some improvements have been made, and features have been added and removed from a different edition of the formatting style. However, when writing an academic paper, it is important to check with your instructor concerning the use of the listing methods.

When listing items, there are three ways to list items in an academic paper, and they include:

The Bulleted List

When a writer wants to draw visual interest without suggesting that the listed items go in a certain direction, the best way to list such items is via the bulleted list. For instance, listing an item that does not have an order of significance or is not in chronological order, the writer can easily make use of the bulleted listing style.

To list items in the bulleted form, the user needs to use the bullet function of their word processing program. Selecting the bullet function will indent the list. There are various shapes the bullet can take, and they include:

- Dots
- Squares
o Small circles and so on.

If items that are bulleted are complete sentences, then it is correct, to begin with, a capital letter and finish with punctuation, normally a period.

For items that are phrases or short words, those are the kind of words that are not considered complete sentences. It is proper to begin them with a lowercase, apart from words that are proper nouns.

When actions are phrases or words, there are two ways they can be punctuated when using the bullet list. The first method is to use no punctuation at the end of the bulleted items, even at the end of the last one. This is preferable for short sentences or phrases.

The second one is to put the punctuations at the end of the sentence as if the bullets were not there, to begin with. This is more suitable for lengthy and complicated sentences.

The Numbered List
Numbered lists are suitable for organizing items, especially when there is a procedure to be followed. It is, however, appropriate to note that using a numbered list may set items in an unnecessary ordinal situation. For example, using the numbered list may connote that the items are in chronological form or that there is an order of importance attached to the items. To avoid this suggestive situation, list the items in a bulleted format.

To use the numbered list function, select the function from your app's processing program, and it will be indented automatically. The numbered list should be identified by an Arabic numeral that is succeeded by a period, it should not be surrounded in, or the following character should not be a parenthesis.

The Lettered List
Sometimes sentences can contain a list of items; when these items number three or more, use a serial comma before the last item. For example, information that was gathered about

the participating groups is their age, gender, and economic status.

But when the items already contain commas, make use of semicolons in the stead of commas. (American Psychological Association, 2020, p. 189).

A lettered list in a sentence is a great way to specify characteristics in succession without breaking the components as obtained in a numbered or bulleted list. To indicate the list within the sentence or paragraph, use lowercase letters within parentheses. (American Psychological Association, 2020, p. 189). For instance, "the laborers were asked to choose between (a) an hourly pay without a bonus, (b) weekly payment without bonus or (c) monthly payments with series of bonuses."

In academic papers, the bulleted and numbered listings are used sparingly because academic paper requires the writer's to display their critical thinking ability. Using the bulleted or numbered lists only provides information in bits rather than include an in-depth analysis.

CHAPTER ELEVEN

Tables And Figures

Tables and figures play an important role whether it is in an academic paper or not. They help the writer present vast amounts of data efficiently, making it more discernible to readers. The goal of tables and figures is to present articles to readers in a more neat and easy to comprehend manner. The best tables are elegant, and tables usually show numerical values such as standard deviation, mean, mode, etc. They can also contain textual information, or contain both, arranged in columns and rows. A figure can be a chart, drawing, photograph, plot, and other descriptions that are not a table. To make tables and figures easy to comprehend, APA has a set of rules writers must follow.

Organization

It is also important to organize tables and figures successively. Other information in the table and figure must be consistent in terms of abbreviation, probability, values.

Tables

Tables are graphic presentations interpreted in columns and rows through which digits, texts, or a mixture of both digits and texts are illustrated. Types of tables include correlation table, analysis of variance table, demographic characteristics table, factor analysis tables, etc.

DATA THAT CAN BE PRESENTED IN TABLE FORMAT.

Suitable data required for table presentation are data that are considered to be complex and cannot be easily understood in their written format. In order to present these kinds of data efficiently, they must be presented logically.

Numbering
Tables should be numbered successively using only Arabic numerals; avoid using suffix letters when numbering a table. For example, it is inappropriate to use Table 1a, 1b, etc. Rather if it includes an appendix with the tables, combine the related tables and identify them with a mixture of capital letters and Arabic numerals, for instance, Table B2, Table C3, etc.

Table Title
Tables should have a title that is clear and concise, and the title should be written below the table in italics.

HEADINGS

Headings should be written in a clear and concise manner. The heading must not be longer than the longest threshold in a column or row. Abbreviations may be used to make the heading fit into the column. There can be a variety of headings depending on how the data are arranged on the table. There are different types of heading.

- Stub heading: this describes the left-hand column that usually lists some major independent variable.

- Column heading depicts the entries below them in just one entry.
- Column spanners are sometimes stacked on top of column headings and together are called decked heads. They are known as the column that describes the entries below them.
- Table spanners cover the entirety of the table; it allows for more division or combination of identical column headings and is the only type of heading that can be plural.

When constructing tables, all columns must have a heading written in a sentence, which must be in the singular form. Also, every column item should be parallel; once a symbol is indicated in the heading, it is unnecessary to repeat it.

Body
The body is the crucial portion of the table, which includes all the data recorded, arranged in cells (i.e., the intersection of row and column). It is important that words are entered in sentence cases, and the words should be center-aligned except in cases where aligning it to the left will make it easier to understand. When there is no available data for a cell, leave it empty; a dash can be used in the cell, and if necessary, a general note can be used to explain the missing data.

When recording data, consistency should be a priority: digits should be communicated to a constant amount of decimal areas defined by the accuracy of distribution. Do not try to alter the calculation of decimal areas in the exact column.

Notes

There are three kinds of notes for a table: the general, the specific notes, and the probability notes. Notes usually appear under the table and explain details that cannot be understood from the available data on the table. Notes can be the definition of abbreviations, attribution of Copyright, and so on.

General Notes: they give information regarding the table as a whole; they explain abbreviations and others.

Specific Notes; as its name implies, it explains data on a specific column or single data entry. When specific notes are to be conveyed, it is vital to use superscript lowercase letters.

Probability Notes; they make known the findings of the tests for statistical significance. The probability notes are only needed when it is pertinent to the data in the table. It is strongly advised to make use of the same asterisk for an assigned alpha level throughout the article.

Borders

The use of borders on a table should be limited to only when it is required for clearness sake. Generally, borders are used at the top or at the foot of the table, above the column spanner, and beneath the column head. Make sure not to use borders to distinguish data and desist from using it in cells of a column.

Figure

In APA, all types of displays that are not tables are considered figures. Figures include bar graphs, line graphs, all types of charts, drawings, infographics, and others.

Numbering

Figures are to be numbered in the decree in which they occur in your paper, and the figure volume must appear above the title and in bold font.

Title

Figures are to have a brief and descriptive title, which is to appear one double-spaced line under the figure number. They are to be capitalized in italics.

Image

Drawings, graphs, photographs are the image part of a figure when the text appears; use san-serif font 8 to 14 points.

Legend

A figure legend is positioned at each figure's border and clarifies any symbol utilized in each figure. Statements in the legend are to be capitalized in the title case.

Notes

Just like in tables, notes appear below the figure and explains or describes words that cannot be easily understood in the presented figures. There are three types of notes, and they are as follows; the general notes, the specific, and the probability notes.

CHAPTER TWELVE

Notes

It has been established that the APA style formatting requires two citations within a paper. First is the citation within the body of the text and on the reference list at the climax of the manuscript. To make an academic paper clear and easy to understand, APA has set guidelines a writer must follow.

How To Cite Lecturers Note In APA Style

Notes from a lecture are deemed personal communication in APA style, they can be cited within the text of an assignment, and that's where it ends. They cannot be added to the reference list. Such citations are to be added immediately after the quote in the following manner (D.D. the instructor, subjective information, month day, the year it took place).

However, handouts that are distributed in class, including PowerPoint presentations and slides, should be cited both in-text and on the reference list.

How to cite personal notes in APA Style

Lecture notes taken in live face-to-face or online classes are considered or known as personal communications. They are considered thus because they cannot be found in any recorded or print format.

In-text citation: (V. Orieke, personal communication, September 22, 2021)

Paraphrase: V. Orieke (personal communication, September 22, 2021) discussed the difference between in-text citation and paraphrasing.

Quotation: According to V. Orieke (personal communication, September 22, 2021), there is a difference between an in-text citation and a paraphrase.

Furthermore, personal communication only has to be cited in-text only; there is no need to add it to the reference list.

CHAPTER THIRTEEN

Appendices

When a writer wants to introduce a piece of additional information that may not fit in within the article's body, the writer can make use of an appendix to make the readers understand better without creating or distracting the flow of the text. In other words, an appendix is a section at the end of a writer's work that incorporates data that couldn't fit into the body of the work.

The primary purpose of appendices is to initiate further research materials, describe specific elements of a study. They are concise and brief and only explain relevant contents. Appendices may require an acknowledgment of Copyright and compliance to privacy policies to safeguard the identities of participating characters when data is cited.

To add an appendix to a paper; there are some rules that must be adhered to in order to meet the APA standards:

- All appendices must appear after the reference list.
- When an author has numerous appendices, they should be named sequentially. For instance, the first should be called appendix A, the next appendix B, and so on.

- All appendix should appear in the order that each data is illustrated in the document.
- Each of the appendices should commence on a fresh page; no two appendices are to be written together.

An appendix is not a compulsory part of a paper, so a writer doesn't always have to include an appendix. Appendices are created to give readers more insight into the main discussion; it aims to provide more information to buttress statements made in the text. However, it is not vital to the contention of the paper. The following may be included in the appendix of a paper:

- Interviews conducted: a writer can include transcripts of interviews conducted in the course of research and data gathering, which can be quoted from the main text.
- Documents used in the research: the author or writer can include documents that were used in the process of the research. These documents can be instructions, questionnaires, scales, and other tests.
- Detailed data: these can be statistical data in their full details that are often presented in tables or figures.
- An author can also include the equipment used in the course of the research and writing of the paper.

It is important that an author refers to each appendix at least once in the main text. An appendix should not be included if it was not referred to in the main text. When an author wants to refer to an appendix, it should be done in this format: (see appendix A for the entire interview transcripts). When referring to the same interviews, mentioning the appendix again is not necessary.

Formatting Appendices
Appendices are created on a separate page called the **appendix,** followed by a title on the following line that illustrates the subject the appendix is aiming to discuss. The headings of the appendix should be centered and bolded at the top-most part of the page with a title case. The appendix should be left-aligned; they must be doubled spaced, with their page numbers at the left-hand corner. In cases where there are multiple appendices, each should have its label with a capital letter and reference in the text by a specific title.

Text Appendices
Appendices may integrate texts, figures, tables, and they should be labeled with the letter of the affiliated appendix followed by the number implying the order in which they come. The appendix should be formatted in conventional paragraph style. If there is only a single appendix in the paper, it should still be labeled with the letter A and a number to distinguish between it and the one existing in the document.

Table Or Figure Appendices
When an appendix contains only a table or figure, the title of the table or figure should be substituted with the title of the appendix. For instance, if appendix C contains only one table or figure, the table or figure should be labeled appendix C and

not Table C3 as obtainable when there are multiple tables and figures.

When an appendix contains many tables and figures without text, it should be formatted like a text appendix and would receive a name and label. The figure and table on the appendix would furthermore be allotted harmonizing letters and numbers. For example, if Appendix B contains two figures and one table, they should be labeled "Figure B1", Figure B2", "Table B1" consecutively.

Does Appendix In APA Style Need Numbering?
When there is more than one appendix in a paper that follows the APA guidelines, they should be labeled as follows: "Appendix A," "Appendix B," etc. It is also important to note that each appendix should start on a different page.

CHAPTER FOURTEEN

Among Others, Including

The 7th Edition of the APA formatting style was introduced in October 2019 to replace the 6th Edition that was published in 2009. Among other things, there were a lot of changes from the 6th Edition. The 7th Edition allowed for more flexibility in terms of citing online sources. The application and use of bias-free and inclusive language have become more important.

The 7th publication addresses all these modifications by giving adequate and detailed actions. The biggest modification in the 7th publication of the APA style is that.

- There is no need to add the publisher in the reference citation.
- There is also another chance in the in-text reference for sources that have more than three authors. Rather than list all the author names as was obtainable in the 6th Edition, in the 7th Edition, you only write the initials of the first authors followed by et al.
- The reference list can now have up to twenty author names and initials. This means that instead of the usual seven, surname and initials of up to twenty authors should be entered into the reference list if available.

- The DOI label is no more important. DOIs are presently formatted as URLs.
- Adding "retrieved from" before URLs is no longer necessary unless instructed otherwise. The writer should include the website title unless it has the exact title of the writer.
- When it comes to eBooks, the structure or the kind of gadget is no longer added to the reference list, but the publisher's name is incorporated.

Language That Is Inclusive And Bias-free
APA's new standard includes writing in a broad and bias-free language. There is a new chapter dedicated to this in APA's new publication.

APA has created guidelines to help authors lessen bias around sensitive issues such as gender, racial and ethnic identity, disabilities, sexual direction, and age. Also, individual portrayal at the ethical level of carefulness. Here are some examples:

- In the 7th Edition of the American Psychological Association's publication, "they" and "their" is now approved as a gender unbiased pronoun.
- Descriptive phrases are now used to describe a group of people instead of using adjectives. For instance, "People living in poverty" and not "the poor."
- Exact age sizes that are more suitable are now selected to broader categories. For example, "people over 30 years" is no longer acceptable. Rather writer should go

for a more specific range, such as individuals in the age range of 30 to 40 years old.

Types Of APA Style Papers

There are two major types of manuscripts that can be written with the APA style, and they include a Literature review and experimental reports. Each of them has a set of guidelines unique to them. APA set that to guide authors.

Literature reviews: this is the summary of what the scientific publications say about your particular questions.

Most literature reviews feature the following:

- Page title
- The Introduction area
- Reference list

However, literary review and annotated biographies are not similar. APA has guidelines for annotated biographies that are different from literature reviews.

Experimental reports: in several social sciences, students can be asked to conduct experimental research. Experimental articles have a more detailed arrangement described in relation to that of the literature review. The APA layout for experimental reports follows a scientific procedure that makes a paper easy to read by incorporating cues for more efficiency. These cues make it easy for readers to scan for information on a paper, and they include:

- The importance of the topic. This information is covered in the introduction.
- Also covered in the introduction is the problem question.
- The steps the writer took to address the problem this is covered in the methods or methodology.
- The outcome or what was found. This is covered in the results section.
- What the writer thinks the findings center upon. This is covered in the discussions section.

Therefore, experimental reports have the following sections:

- The title
- The next chapter would be Abstracts
- Then Introduction
- Followed by methods
- Then the outcomes or results
- The discussion about the findings
- The References list
- Appendices
- Tables or figures if necessary

Other Papers

When submitting a paper to a publication, ensure to make use of the guidelines stated in the publication, and include as many sections you think are acceptable to submitting your publication. But endeavor to keep your readers in mind.

The Basic Rule Of Reference Lists

Reference should emerge at the end of a manuscript, and it should deliver the crucial data a reader may require if they wish to fetch a source referred to in the body of the manuscript. Every citation in the document must be duly listed in the reference, and every all admissions in the reference list must be referred to in the text.

The reference list should begin on a fresh page different from that of the manuscript. The page should be labeled "References" at the top and center of the sheet. The title shouldn't be bolded, and quotation marks shouldn't be used on it.

- All the lines succeeded by the initial line of the entrance when referencing should be indented one-half of an inch from the left edge. This is known as the hanging indentation.
- In APA style referencing, the names of authors are reversed; the last name comes first. Write the last name and initials for all participating authors on the referenced work; you can add up to twenty authors. In cases where there are more than twenty authors, write the last names and initials of nineteen authors, then use ellipses after the nineteenth writer. After using the ellipses, write the name and initials of the last author. Initially, in the 6th Edition of the APA guideline, you could only add seven authors.
- Entrance in a reference list should be alphabetically using the first author's last name of the particular work.

- In situations where there are extra articles by the same writer, either single-author references or numerous writer references with precisely the same authors in the exact same order are listed by the year it was published, starting with the earlier one.
- In journal titles, writers must capitalize all manor words.
- The title of papers of long nature, such as books and journals, should be italicized.
- Desist from underlining, italicizing, or adding quotations around the titles of edited short works like articles, journals.

Citing Indirect Sources

When referencing an article that was cited in another source, add the actual quotation in your signal phrase and note the secondary source in your reference list; include the source in the parentheses.

For electronic sources, try as much as possible to cite them as you would cite any other documents using the author-date style.

When the author is unknown, and the date is missing, make use of the title in the signal phrase, or initial statement, or two titles from work in parentheses and add the letters (n.d), which means there is no date.

APA PAPER FORMAT

In the 7th Edition, paper format guidelines for student and professional papers are now different. Some changes worthy of note include:

- There is now a more flexible approach to the use of fonts. Options now include Calibri, Arial, Georgia, Times New Roman, etc.
- The word " Running head" is no longer included in the running head of the title page. It now only contains the page number and a paper title.
- The running head has also been removed from the student's papers unless instructed otherwise by the student's instructor.

Technicalities Of Style
When it comes to style, only a few changes were made. These changes include:

- Only one space after a period at the end of a sentence is now required.
- Using italics to refer to linguistics is no longer required; instead, make use of quotation marks.

Why Is APA Style Needed?
APA style creates uniformity and consistency that helps readers to focus on the message and ideas that the authors are trying to pass. Instead of just scanning through for key points.

APA guidelines help authors avoid inconsistencies, omissions in punctuations, in-text citations, references, and other distractions. Distractions that will prevent readers from getting essential information from the paper. Using APA guideline make ideas to flow logically, and ensures appropriate acknowledgment of sources and papers organized consistently.

Conclusion

The 7th Edition of the APA formatting style brings changes to how referencing should be done. These changes make it different from the previous Edition. For instance, you can now write the names of up to 20 authors in a reference list, and words like "retrieved from" are no longer necessary. The importance of the APA formatting manual is to help users acquire adequate writing methods, and both students and professionals can use this manual.

This manual is to guide users on how to properly cite sources in ways that make them clear and easy for readers to understand. Additionally, it aims to help students and professionals alike accomplish eminence and superiority in their publications.

Made in the USA
Las Vegas, NV
12 October 2023

78994331R00046